❀ This book is about ❀

....

My SCOTTISH ANCESTRY

Create A Lasting Record Of Your Ancestors

Helen Tovey

Introduction

Scotland's history is world-renowned, its culture treasured and its scenery breath-taking and if you are lucky enough to have Scottish blood running through your veins, you will find the trip back to the past to find your ancestors enthralling.

The population of Scotland today is only five million, but an estimated 30 million people globally claim Scottish ancestry, the Scottish diaspora.

Tracing your family history is absorbing, although it can seem confusing too. Luckily Scotland has some of the most extensive records of its inhabitants in years gone by, which will help to make your journey back to the past easier.

Vast collections of records can be found in local and national archives. Websites, too, will provide access to records, sometimes free of charge, other times for a fee. The internet has made some of the historical documents you will need to search much quicker and easier to use, perhaps saving you time and money too. However, it has by no means replaced traditional research, and if you have the opportunity to visit places in Scotland on the trail of your ancestors you should seize the chance.

Besides the official government records (such as those of births, marriages and deaths, and the censuses), you may also have family tales to help give you clues. Memories such as these are to be treasured. On the journey to find your ancestors you will be learning so much more than simply names and dates, although these are the starting point. You will be unearthing the story of your family, and very likely discovering ways of life in bygone times, old occupations, lost languages, times of hardship and brilliance, in the rich tapestry of your Scottish ancestors' lives.

Contents ⚘

Getting Started

Where do you start with your family history?
You start with yourself. Then work back
through the generations, gathering clues from
family stories, relatives' memories, old letters,
photo albums, memorabilia and mementoes.
You will be surprised at the clues you reveal,
once you start looking.

❧

Where To Begin

To make a start researching your family history, write down details that you can remember about your own life. Then do the same for your parents and grandparents, enlisting their help if possible. You may find that older relatives can be a rich source of names, dates, places and anecdotes. Family history is surprisingly absorbing and you may end up with a mountain of information about your ancestors. For this reason, it is a good idea to keep your notes in good order right from the start.

Set up a folder (on paper or your computer), allowing a page or file per person. You will soon add to this, but your family history is likely to grow in unexpected directions, so it helps to keep your notes in a flexible format.

Use these lines to provide more information about these photographs

....

....

Place your photo(s) here

Use this space for some of your favourite family photos

Family Record Sheet

In addition, it can be handy to use a sheet of paper per couple. On it you can store brief details for the couple, their parents and their children, making them easy to view at a glance. Use the layout below as a guide for your family record sheet.

Husband _____							
Born:							
Baptised:							
Married:							
Died:							
Buried:							
Occupation:							
Father:							
Mother:							
Census:							
1841	1851	1861	1871	1881	1891	1901	1911

Wife _____							
Born:							
Baptised:							
Married:							
Died:							
Buried:							
Occupation:							
Father:							
Mother:							
Census:							
1841	1851	1861	1871	1881	1891	1901	1911

	Children	Born/Baptised	Married	Died/Buried	Census 1841	1851	1861	1871	1881	1891	1901	1911
1												
2												
3												
4												
5												
6												
7												
8												

Reference & Notes:

Prepared by: ....

The Family Tree

*O*nce you have collected some names and dates, it is a good idea to start drawing up a family tree. Your tree will be really helpful, both showing the ancestors you have found as well as the gaps for the people you still need to find. Don't worry about writing out your tree beautifully, but it does need to be legible. There are also a few conventions that people tend to use when filling in their family trees, which help to keep it easy to make sense of.

To create a standard family tree (a pedigree chart), take a large sheet of paper. If you write it in pencil, you will be able to make changes easily. Write your own name in the centre, near the bottom of the sheet. Then write your parents' names above that, with your father's name above and to the left of your name and your mother's to the right.

Adding in brief dates, such as for birth, marriage and death, will help to clarify who is who. This can be particularly useful in families that used the same first names generation after generation. Continue adding people, working back through the generations, with the male of each couple to the left-hand side, and the female to the right. Traditionally an equal (=) sign is used between them, to show that they are married. If someone marries twice, put a small number one, two etc in a circle, to denote which is the first spouse, etc.

If you prefer you may also buy paper family tree charts to fill in, or use a family history program on your computer. Look out for family history websites, which you can use to build an online tree; there are some free of charge sites for doing this around.

Tip

The members of each generation should always be placed in line with each other horizontally on your family tree chart, so that you can easily read across it to see who all your grandparents are, for instance.

Pedigree Chart

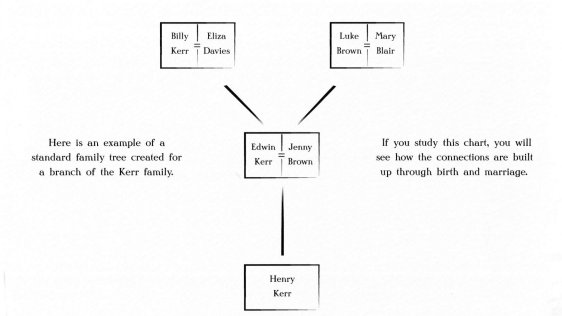

Here is an example of a standard family tree created for a branch of the Kerr family.

If you study this chart, you will see how the connections are built up through birth and marriage.

My Family Tree

Using the space below, a pencil, ruler and some neat handwriting, practise sketching out a simple family tree from the information you wrote down on page 7.

Asking Questions

You may be very lucky and have old family photo albums, letters, journals and artefacts, and perhaps even a family bible handed down through the generations. These treasured heirlooms will help you learn about your family's past. However, do not forget your living relatives, both those closer to home and more distant ones, as their memories are to be valued too. Family historians often regret not asking more questions, as relatives can often reveal so much more than official records.

You could ask your relatives whether they would be willing to fill in a questionnaire, or perhaps be interviewed by you. If you are not regularly in contact with them, it would be courteous to write in the first instance, to gauge their response. Not everyone is willing to talk about the past; perhaps they have private matters that they would rather not share.

However, hopefully you will find that many of your relatives, both the elderly and those not so old, will be only too happy to reminisce about years gone by, providing you with a wealth of details and possible leads and anecdotes to enrich your family history. Make sure you keep careful notes, perhaps recording the interviews too. If necessary double-check the details with them at a later date, to ensure you have written everything down correctly.

You could also organize a family reunion: a chance for your relatives to get together, bake family recipes, and share family photos and stories. Don't forget to display your family tree.

TIP
Sources help to prove that your family history is based on research, not wishful thinking, so keep a careful note of them. Sources might be a document's reference number or may simply show that you got the information from your granny, uncle, etc.

My Family Treasures

Use the space below for a favourite anecdote or treasured photos of your ancestors.

....
....
....
....
....
....
....
....

Place a photo, postcard
or clipping here

Place a photo, postcard
or clipping here

TIP

Why not scan in your family photos
and email copies to relatives. Ask
them to do the same, and not only
will you gain new photos for your
collection, but you now have a
back-up in case anything should
happen to the original.

Researching Names & Clans ✦

Your surname can reveal a great deal about your ancestors, and will be essential to tracing your family history. The more uncommon your surname is, the easier it makes your search. Gaelic, Norse, and Norman influences added to the linguistic mix from which Scottish surnames developed, as did others, such as

the Picts, Anglians, Britons and most recently Irish. Surnames came into use from the twelfth century in Scotland, but they continued to evolve and have variations into the nineteenth century.

Although it is possible, a shared surname by no means indicates a shared ancestry; it is your research that will help you work out who your ancestors are. In addition, DNA tests are increasingly being used to help determine which people with a shared surname are related to one another by blood.

Clans are particular to the Scottish Highlands and to some prestigious Borders families too, and they arose as people sought to protect their territories. Not everyone with the same clan surname has a shared ancestry – they may have simply adopted the name to indicate their allegiance. Equally there are also people within the same clan, who may have different surnames too.

Official clans are registered with the Court of the Lord Lyon, and include famous names such as Campbell, MacDonald, Robertson and Stewart. Many of the clan names are still widely in use in Scotland today.

Another important element for Scottish clans is their tartan, which has had a controversial history. After the Battle of Culloden in 1746, the English government forbade the wearing of tartan by Highland men until 1782, to discourage clan identity and unity. It was not until the early 1800s that the association of clans, surnames and tartans became closely linked, but in the past two centuries, tartan and clan connections have become known and treasured as a central part of Scottish history.

DID YOU KNOW?

The Scottish tradition for first names is to name the first son after the paternal grandfather, the second after the maternal grandfather, and the third after the father. The same goes for daughters, following the pattern of maternal grandmother's name first, then paternal grandmother, and after that the mother. This reoccurrence of names can be confusing, but can give you clues for names to look out for too.

My Surname

Use the space below to note down any information gathered about your surname.

Surname ....

Origins ....

Meaning ....

Other information ....

....

The Next Steps

Once you have discovered all the details that you and your relatives can remember, then you will need to begin searching the official public records. You can use these records both to double-check the information your family has provided, and to find out new details as well.

As a family historian looking for Scottish ancestors, you are very fortunate, as the key records that you need to start searching are largely online, detailed and comprehensive.

❧

Births, Marriages & Deaths ❧

The statutory registers of births, marriages and deaths are kept by the General Register Office for Scotland and will be invaluable to your research. The earliest of these records date from 1 January 1855. These records are the building blocks of your family history, and you can use the details you find on them, to work back through the generations. There are variations in the actual details recorded, but below is an outline of the sorts of details you can expect to find.

Using Certificates

A Scottish birth register entry can tell you details such as the first and surname of the baby, the full date and time of the birth, the place of birth, full name and occupation of the father, full name and maiden name of the mother, and the date and place of their marriage, and the name of the informant.

You may then use the parents' marriage date and mother's maiden name to find the parents' marriage in the registers too.

A Scottish marriage register entry can tell you details such as the date and place of marriage, whether banns were called, the names, ages, occupations and marital status of the bride and groom, the address of their usual residence, the names and occupations of the couple's fathers, and the names, including maiden names, of their mothers. The register will also state whether a parent is deceased, and will cite the names of the officiating minister and the witnesses.

A Scottish death register entry will tell you the name of the deceased, the date, place and time of death, age at death, the names and occupations of the deceased's parents and whether they too have died, the name of the spouse, the cause of death, and the name and relationship of the informant.

You can search the registers at *www.scotlandspeople.gov.uk* for the years 1855–2006. Images of the earlier register entries are viewable online (birth register images 1855–1910, marriage register images 1855–1935 and death register images 1855–1960).

You will need to buy credits to use this website. For your family history research, it is likely that the birth, marriage or death register image you need to view is online, providing you with full details of the birth, marriage or death, but if you are searching in more recent times, then you may need to order a registered copy – a certificate – from the General Register Office for Scotland. There is a charge for this service.

When civil registration was introduced in Scotland in 1855, 1,027 registration districts were established in the country, and they roughly equated to the existing 900 parishes in Scotland at the time.

Scots have always been an adventurous lot, so you may need to search overseas records. If you are trying to trace the birth, marriage or death of a British citizen or subject, which took place overseas, try the High Commission, consular, and Army birth, marriage and death indexes.

BMD Record Sheets

Using a record sheet like the one shown here, you can begin to piece together the important events in each for your ancestors' lives from the information you gather from their birth, marriage and death certificates.

Name ....

Relationship to you ....

Birth Certificate

• *GROS reference* ....

• *Full name* ....

• *Date of birth* ....

• *Place of birth* ....

• *Sex* ....

• *Mother's name* ....

• *Mother's maiden name* ....

• *Father's name* ....

• *Father's occupation* ....

Informant:

• *Name* ....

• *Address* ....

• *Relationship to child* ....

Marriage Certificate

- GROS reference ....
- Full name ....
- Date of marriage ....
- Place of marriage ....
- Age ....
- Marital status ....
- Occupation ....
- Address ....
- Father's name ....
- Father's occupation ....
- Names of the witnesses ....
....

Spouse:
- Name ....
- Age ....
- Marital status ....
- Occupation ....
- Address ....
- Father's name ....
- Father's occupation ....

Death Certificate

- GROS reference ....
- Full name ....
- Date of death ....
- Place of death ....
- Sex ....
- Age/date of birth ....
- Occupation ....
- Cause of death ....

Informant:
- Name ....
- Address ....
- Relationship to deceased ....

You may want to leave space at the bottom of each record sheet for any further information obtained from the certificates.

Other information ....
....
....

Census Returns ✸

ensus returns were not made with family historians in mind, but they are extremely useful in family history research. The census gives a snapshot of the population, once a decade, listing everyone according to household. For most of our ancestors, we should be able to find them listed in the census returns, with their full name, age, occupation, place of birth and address.

TIP
When you find a relative, make a careful note of the document reference. This comprises: the series number, piece number, folio number and page number. This enables you to return to the document easily, and to provide a source reference for your family history.

Bear in mind that for the 1841 census (but not later ones) the age of people over 15 was rounded to the nearest five years. From 1851 onwards the relationship to the head of the household, of each person in that household, is recorded on the census. If your ancestor was born in Scotland, the exact place will be given. However, if your ancestor was born overseas, then the form may simply cite the country, which can be frustratingly vague.

What Is Available

The census is particularly important when tracing your family ancestry, as it includes everyone, adults and children, regardless of their wealth or status in society, whereas many other historical documents only deal with a certain group of people for instance, voters, militia, etc.

Searching the census can reveal a particular insight to your family, as it will show the other family members, such as your direct ancestors' siblings. By working back through the censuses you will get a feel for an ancestor's family – babies born, children sadly dying, others growing up and leaving home, changes of address and occupation. You may also note widows and widowers and second marriages. These details, briefly recorded on the census will help you to try to imagine the domestic lives that your ancestors led.

Viewing The Records

The first census of use to family historians, being widely available, and providing individuals' names, is the 1841 census. This and subsequent censuses, up to 1911, are available for searching. You may search the indexes and view images of the original census returns online at *www.scotlandspeople.gov.uk*. This is the official government site, but there are other websites that provide transcriptions and indexes of some of the Scottish censuses, such as *www.ancestry.com* and *www.freecen.org.uk*.

TIP
As the census is supposed to be a record of the entire population it can be extremely frustrating if you cannot find your ancestor. This is the time when your family history detective skills will have to come into play. Did a boundary change? Did they move house? Were they overseas or even in prison? Or there could simply be a spelling mistake in the records. If you find an ancestor in one census, but they are not in the subsequent one, it is worth checking the death records, in case they have died in the intervening years. Unfortunately there are a few small gaps in the census records.

Page 42] The undermentioned Houses are situate within the Boundaries of the

*Civil Parish of Wilton	Quoad sacra Parish of	Parliamentary Burgh of Hawick	Royal Burgh of	Police Burgh of	Town of	Village or Hamlet

No. of Schedule	ROAD, STREET, &c., and No. or NAME of HOUSE.	HOUSES.	NAME and Surname of each Person.	RELATION to Head of Family.	CONDITION.	AGE of Males	AGE of Females	Rank, Profession, or OCCUPATION.	WHERE BORN.	Whether 1. Deaf and Dumb. 2. Blind. 3. Imbecile or Idiot. 4. Lunatic.	
195	Newstead	1	Samuel McGee	Head	Mar	36		Mason (Journeyman)	Roxburghshire Wilton		
			Mary Ann Do	Wife	Mar		28		Dumfriesshire Lockmaben		
			James Do	Son		2			Roxburghshire Wilton		
			Christy Thomson	Boarder	Mar		41		Do Hawick		
			Margaret Chisholm	Boarder	unm		17	Tweed Picker	Do Hawick		
196	Do		Andrew Butler	Head	Mar	31		Wool Frame Work Knitter	Roxburghshire Wilton		
			Agnes Do	Wife	Mar		24		Do Hawick		
			William Do	Son		1			Do Wilton		
197	Do	1	James McGee	Head	Mar	50		Wool Frame Work Knitter	Ireland		
			Janet Do	Wife	Mar		55		Roxburghshire Cavers		
			Margaret Do	Daur	unm		23	Wool Frame Loom Weaver	Do Wilton		
			Elizabeth Do	Daur	unm		18	Do Do	Do Do		
			Janet Do	James Daur			4		Do Do		
			George Thomson	Father in law	Wid	81		Wool Frame Work Knitter	Do Do		
198	Do		William Snayden	Head	Mar	23		Wool Frame Work Knitter	Roxburghshire Wilton		
			Jane Do	Wife	Mar		21				
199	Do		James Laidon	Head	Mar	56		Wool Handloom Weaver	Roxburghshire Wilton		
			Helen Do	Wife	Mar		58		Dumfriesshire Dumfries		
			James Do	Son	unm	20		Wool Spinner	Roxburghshire Wilton		
			Agnes Do	Daur	unm		18	Wool Frame Loom Weaver	Do Do		
			Alexander Do	Son	unm	16		Do Do Spinner	Do Do		
	Total of Houses ..	2			Total of Males and Females ..	10	11		Total of Children receiving Instruction, and Windowed Rooms ..	6	

* Draw the pen through such of the words as are inappropriate.

When searching the census records you will be using the enumerators' summary books (sometimes abbreviated to ESBs). It was the enumerator's duty to collate all the information that he had collected from households in his enumeration district. This is why you see details for several households on a sheet – it is the enumerator's list.

Recording Census Information

By using a record sheet like the one shown below, you can begin to gather some more detailed information about each of your ancestors and members of their families from the census returns.

Name ....

Relationship to you ....

- *Forename* ....

- *Surname* ....

- *Address* ....

- *Relationship to head of family* ....

- *Marital status* ....

- *Age* ....

- *Sex* ....

- *Profession or occupation* ....

- *Birthplace* ....

- *Disabilities* ....

- *Relationships/family members* ....

    ....

    ....

    ....

    ....

    ....

Parish Registers

*O*nce you get back to the mid-1800s, to trace your ancestors further back in time, you will now need to look to the Old Parish Registers (OPRs), to find details of your ancestors' births, baptisms, banns and marriages, and burials.

The earliest Old Parish Registers date from the sixteenth century, but records for many parishes did not exist until much later – the late eighteenth century. It was not compulsory to register a baptism or marriage with the parish, so whether an event was recorded in the parish register is partly down to individual choice and to the diligence of the parish priest. Baptisms, proclamations of banns and marriages are most often recorded, and burials less so.

You will find that the level of detail in the parish registers is far less than that for the civil registration records you will have searched. Nevertheless, for finding ancestors before the mid-1800s, the Old Parish Registers will be your key tool.

Searching The Registers

The website *www.scotlandspeople.gov.uk* gives access to the Old Parish Registers, 1538–1854, for births and baptisms, banns and marriages and burials. As mentioned previously, the records available will vary between parishes. You will need to buy credits to view the registers on this site, but this will enable you to view scanned images of the original pages. Old Parish Register births and baptisms, *c.* 1564–1950, and marriages *c.* 1561–1910, can be searched free of charge at *www.familysearch.org*. The collection is periodically added to, but by no means includes all the OPRs.

TIP

The OPRs are the registers kept by the Church of Scotland parishes, so if your ancestor was of another denomination or religion you will need to search in other registers. Some of the Roman Catholic registers are online at *www.scotlandspeople.gov.uk*, and there are also Free Church, Baptist and Jewish records to consider, for instance.

Parish Record Sheet

The level of detail in a birth or baptism entry in the register will vary. Sometimes both the dates of birth and baptism are included. You can also find the child's name, father's name and occupation, mother's name and maiden name (although sometimes the mother's name will be left out altogether), place of residence, and names of witnesses.

These baptism details will enable you to look for your parents' marriage entry in the OPRs too, so that you can work back through the generations.

The details available for an OPR marriage may include, date of marriage, place of residence, the names of the bride and groom, and perhaps the groom's occupation and the name of the bride's father.

Recording Parish Information

Baptism Records

• *Date of baptism* ....

• *Child's name* ....

• *Father's name* ....

• *Mother's name* ....

• *Name of church* ....

• *Parish* ....

• *Other information* ....

....

....

....

....

....

Marriage Records

- *Name* ....
- *Marital status* ....
- *Spouse's name* ....
- *Spouse's marital status* ....
- *Date of marriage* ....
- *Name of church* ....
- *Parish* ....
- *Other information* ....

....

....

....

Burial Records

- *Name* ....
- *Date of burial* ....
- *Name of church* ....
- *Parish* ....
- *Other information* ....

....

....

....

Other Records

(e.g. tombstone inscriptions, etc.)

....

....

....

Building a Picture

The birth, marriage, death and census records, and the Old Parish Registers will have helped provide you with the information to draw up your family tree. However, you will also have found intriguing snippets and other clues that you will wish to research further, to help you understand the past and enrich your family history. On the pages that follow are suggestions of records that might help you build a picture of the past.

❧

Wills & Testaments

Although the majority of Scottish people in centuries past did not leave a will or testament, when you do find an ancestor in the records, the details can be quite revealing.

When a person died leaving a will, the testament (the document that resulted once the executor had been approved by the court) was known as the 'testament testamentar'. This included among other things a copy of the will and an inventory of goods. A 'will' comprises the written wishes of the deceased, regarding the disposal of their possessions and naming the executor. Importantly wills tend to name family members, and possibly friends to whom they have left their possessions. Often the oldest son will not be mentioned in a will, because he inherited the land and property. An inventory related to all the moveable property of the deceased, but the details you will find will vary – from a brief mention of the total value of the goods, to an itemised list of possessions. However, if a person died intestate – without a will – the testament was known as the 'testament dative'. The key details, for family historians, in this instance, will be in the inventory.

There were several noticeable laws and traditions surrounding Scottish wills and testaments. Until 1868 only moveable property was able to be included in a Scottish will. From 1868 wills were increasingly used to transfer goods and property.

Where To Find Them

Before 1823 testaments were recorded in the commissary court for that parish, but from 1824 onwards commissary courts were replaced by the sheriff courts, though the process of change was gradual, over several years.

An index of 611,000 wills and testaments, dating from 1500 to 1901, is accessible on *www.scotlandspeople.gov.uk*. To view digital images of the documents you will need to place an order online or visit the ScotlandsPeople Centre.

DID YOU KNOW?
The moveable property (everything from tools to jewels, furniture and clothes) was divided equally into thirds: one third for the wife – the widow's part, one third among the remaining children – the bairns' part, and one third according to the will of the deceased – the deid's part.

Military Records

There are many famous Scottish regiments and servicemen, and many people will come across ancestors who served in the First and Second World Wars, and in earlier times too. It can be moving and fascinating to find out about your ancestors' years in the Armed Forces, and, with luck, you should be able to find out a great deal, as comprehensive, detailed service and pension records were kept.

1914 1918

IN GRATITUDE TO ALL
WHO SERVED, AND IN HONOUR
OF THE PEOPLE OF THIS BOROUGH
WHO FELL IN THE GREAT WARS.
THEY GAVE THEMSELVES
FOR FREEDOM'S CAUSE
THEIR MEMORY NEVER DIES

1939 · 1945

What Is Accessible

The National Archives, Kew, London, holds the majority of the military records for our ancestors from England, Wales, Scotland and Ireland, for the Army, Royal Navy and emerging Royal Air Force, up to the end of the First World War. The archive's website, *www.nationalarchives.gov.uk*, has a catalogue that you can search online, while *www.nationalarchives.gov.uk/documentsonline* has some collections of digitised military records, such as medal index cards. The Commonwealth War Graves Commission has free access to First and Second World War rolls of honour; see *www.cwcg.org*.

Other online records include the soldiers' service and pension records, 1760–1913, which are accessible at *www.findmypast.co.uk*; while the surviving service and pension records for 1914–21 are at *www.ancestry.co.uk*. The originals of all these records are held in the archives at Kew.

For the Second World War, the next of kin (or another person with a letter of authority from the next of kin) may order a copy of the service records of their ancestor, who served in the British Army, Royal Navy or Royal Air Force. It costs £30 to order a copy and you need to apply in writing to the historical disclosures centres (*see* page 43).

The range of records in which to search for your military ancestor is extensive, and in addition to the records mentioned above includes muster rolls, regimental histories, operational war diaries, Army Lists and Navy Lists, and rolls of honour.

DID YOU KNOW?

The National War Museum of Scotland, housed in Edinburgh Castle, has all sorts of information on Scottish regiments. *www.nms.ac.uk/our_museums/war_museum.aspx*.

Everyday Life

*I*n family history, you will find that there is a vast and fascinating range of historic records for discovering more about your ancestors' lives and the times in which they lived. As well as finding out about your ancestors, you may also wish to discover more about their towns, villages, and neighbourhoods.

TIP
Some of the historic records that you would like to search will have been transcribed, but at other times you will find that you need to read old handwriting. This can seem very confusing, but there is a free tutorial at *www.scottishhandwriting.com*.

Maps

When looking at historical records, you might find that you are not familiar with the local place names and area boundaries, so a little time getting the lie of the land will be well spent. Although many of the 33 historic county names are still used colloquially – and will certainly crop up in the censuses and other records in which to search for your ancestors – strictly speaking there are no longer any counties in Scotland. They are now defined as 32 council areas. Having some knowledge of the local geography, and access to historic maps of the areas which your ancestors came from will help you spot that a complete change of place name, may have only meant that your ancestor moved to the next village in the adjacent county, or maybe the boundary simply changed.

Directories

Historic directories are also useful in helping to place your ancestor. They are published more frequently than the census, and if you are lucky, you may find your ancestor listed, perhaps under their occupation in the trade listings, or by their address. Directories add a great deal of colour to our understanding, with descriptions of the local area, and details such as local leisure societies, pillars of the community and more. In more recent times, you may find searching phone directories useful.

Newspapers

Newspapers are another source that may shed light on your ancestors' lives with news items and obituaries. The National Library of Scotland holds many runs, and the British Library Newspapers collection in London has Scottish newspapers too. Local record offices may hold a copy of the local historic newspapers.

Tax and voting records

Tax records, such as valuation rolls and hearth tax records, mention the names of the owner or tenant of each property, so can help you find some ancestors' names. The electoral rolls, are also useful, but again do not list the entire population, only those eligible to vote. The valuation rolls from 1855 are planned to come online at *www.scotlandspeople.gov.uk* soon.

DID YOU KNOW?

A vast collection of 20,000 digitised maps, dating from 1560 to the present day, can be searched at *www.nls.uk/maps* or you may visit the Map Library itself at the National Library of Scotland. The National Library of Scotland has also made many Scottish directories available online and the online collection is growing.

Where To Look Next

One of the many pleasures of researching your family history is that you will find yourself acquiring all sorts of knowledge and skills that will be invaluable in your detective work to see through the mists of time, and travel back on the fascinating journey to find your ancestors.

TIP
Finding an ancestor's grave can be a moving experience. Why not search to see whether the memorial inscriptions have been transcribed for the area in which your ancestor died, so that you can visit the grave and pay your respects.

Kirk Session Records

The Old Parish Registers are just some of the records kept by the parish. Since the Reformation each parish has also had a Kirk Session, which helped to maintain order in the village. These records can provide a useful insight into village life in the past, and you may also find your ancestor's name recorded – perhaps in a neighbourly dispute, for having a child out of wedlock, for witchcraft, and in times of poverty. The originals of the Kirk Session records are held in the National Archives of Scotland, but some of the records, 1501–1900, are due to become available online at *www.scotlandspeople.gov.uk* through 2011 and 2012.

The Kirk Session worked with the local landowners (the heritors) who were bound to contribute to the maintenance of the local church and school, to stipends for the local schoolmaster (the dominie) and minister, and to the poor law.

Further suggestions

Everyone's family is different, and so are our ancestors. On the journey back to the past, you will find that you come across all sorts of opportunities and predicaments faced by your ancestors, and many of these will have left some sort of record. Perhaps you will find yourself searching school records and log books to learn about their childhood years, or maybe looking in adoption records for a long-lost child. For ancestors in more recent times you may find the 1939 National Identity Register (taken at the outbreak of the Second World War as a record of the entire population) useful. Other avenues to search for ancestors could include records for divorce, criminals, emigration, passenger lists, and businesses.

TIP
See the Scottish Archive Network website, *www.scan.org.uk* for an online directory of contact details for more than 50 Scottish archives, and search the online catalogue, which includes details of 20,000 collections from these archives.

Resources

When on the trail of your ancestors you will find yourself searching high and low for gems of information and missing clues. As more and more records become available on the internet, you will find that tracing your family history will become more convenient from wherever you are in the world. With the extensive range of records already online for Scotland you are particularly lucky, but there are still many records solely available in archives.

❦

Useful Websites

*H*ere is a selection of websites that will help you continue your research. You will need to pay to use some of them, but others will provide free information. Some of the sites will be dedicated solely to Scotland, while others will include links and databases covering other countries too. The main port of call, which you are likely to find yourself using to research your Scottish ancestors online is *www.scotlandspeople.gov.uk*.

- www.ancestralscotland.com – genealogy site for the Scottish Tourist Board.

- www.ancestry.co.uk – records include transcripts for Scottish censuses 1841–1901 and First World War service records.

- www.asgra.co.uk – Association of Scottish Genealogists and Record Agents.

- www.censusfinder.com/scotland.htm – links to various census records for Scotland.

- www.cwgc.org – Commonwealth War Graves Commission roll of honour for the First and Second Wars.

- www.familysearch.org – Global family history records, including Scottish ones, such as Old Parish Register baptism and marriage records.

- www.findmypast.com – records include soldiers' service records 1760–1913.

- www.freecen.org.uk – partial transcriptions of the census returns 1841–91.

- www.freereg.org.uk – a limited range of baptism, marriage and burial register transcriptions.

- www.gazettes-online.co.uk – Edinburgh Gazette.

- www.genuki.org.uk – genealogical information for England, Ireland, Wales and, of course, Scotland.

- www.gro-scotland.gov.uk/famrec – General Register Office for Scotland.

- www.mytimemachine.co.uk/scottisharchives.htm – directory of record offices.

- **www.nas.gov.uk** – National Archives of Scotland.

- **www.nationalarchives.gov.uk/documentsonline** – digitised records from The National Archives, London.

- **www.nls.uk** – National Library of Scotland, including beautiful collection of historic online maps and directories.

- **www.nms.ac.uk** – National Museums of Scotland.

- **www.safhs.org.uk** – The Scottish Association of Family History Societies.

- **www.scan.org.uk** – online catalogue for more than 50 Scottish archives.

- **www.scotlandsfamily.com** – aims to provide links to free information and records.

- **www.scotlandspeople.gov.uk** – official website to search for records of ancestors in Scotland, including Old Parish Registers, birth, marriage and death indexes, censuses and wills.

- **www.scotlandspeoplehub.gov.uk** – information on the ScotlandsPeople Centre.

- **www.scotlandsplaces.gov.uk** – information includes county and parish maps.

- **www.scotsdictionaries.org.uk** – resources for the Scots language.

- **www.scotsgenealogy.com** – Scottish Genealogy Society.

- **www.scottishhandwriting.com** – online palaeography tutorials in Scottish handwriting.

- **www.tartanregister.gov.uk** – Scottish register of tartan designs.

- **www.ukbmd.org.uk** – links to sites with birth, marriage and death indexes for areas in the UK.

- **www.undiscoveredscotland.co.uk/usfeatures/timeline/index.html** – timeline of Scottish history.

TIP
Remember that the web is continually growing,
so if you don't find the records you want
online, it is worth revisiting sites from time to time,
to check for new additions.

Useful Addresses
& Further Reading

Below are a selection of addresses for archives and libraries that you may wish to visit, or write to, in the course of your family history research.

When planning your trip, it is always worth contacting the archive or library in advance to double-check opening hours, and to see whether you need to book a seat and bring any identification with you (so that you can get a reader's ticket). This is also a good time to enquire about bringing a laptop and camera – many archives allow the use of these nowadays.

Many archives have online catalogues, so search them to find the details of the records you need. This can save you valuable time on the day, and is particularly useful in case you need to order any records in advance.

Places To Visit

ScotlandsPeople Centre
HM General Register House
2 Princes Street
Edinburgh
EH1 3YY
www.scotlandspeoplehub.gov.uk
0131 314 4300
The ScotlandsPeople Centre will be your main port of call for searching family history records, where, for a daily search fee, you can search all the records on the ScotlandsPeople website, but with valuable additions, such as birth, marriage and death records up to current times, and immediate access to scanned images of the original wills. There are plans to merge the National Archives of Scotland and the General Register Office for Scotland.

National Library of Scotland
George IV Bridge
Edinburgh
EH1 1EW
www.nls.uk
This is Scotland's largest library. In addition it also provides impressive collections of historic maps and directories free to view from its website. The collection of directories is growing and there is a dedicated Scottish Post Office Directories website planned.

Glasgow City Archives
The Mitchell
North Street
Glasgow
G3 7DN
www.glasgow.gov.uk/en/Residents/
Library_Services/The_Mitchell
0141 287 2999 or 2876
Glasgow's archive of records for schools,
businesses, poor law, sasines (land ownership),
police and churches, plus medieval manuscripts,
and collections of photographs and maps.

The National Archives
Kew
Richmond
Surrey
TW9 4DU
www.nationalarchives.gov.uk
020 8876 3444
Military records for the British and Irish armed
forces, whether English, Welsh, Irish or
Scottish are held in here. Search the site
catalogue to view the full range, and also see
the online records at:
www.nationalarchives.gov.uk/documentsonline

Lastly there are three addresses to order more
recent armed service records from:

Army Personnel Centre
Historic Disclosures
Mailpoint 555
Kentigern House
65 Brown Street
Glasgow
G2 8EX
(for Army service records 1939 onwards)

DN Pers
Disclosure Cell
MP G-2
Room 48
West Battery
Whale Island
Portsmouth
PO2 8DX
(for Royal Navy service records 1924
onwards)

RAF Disclosures Section
Room 221b
Trenchard Hall
RAF Cranwell
Sleaford
Lincolnshire
NG34 8HB
(for RAF service records, for officers 1922
onwards and airmen 1924 onwards)

Some Further Reading

Bruce Durie, *Scottish Genealogy,* The History
Press, 2010

*Tracing Your Scottish Ancestors, the Official
Guide,* The National Archives of Scotland and
Birlinn Ltd, 2009

Chris Paton, *Researching Scottish Family
History*, The Family History Partnership, 2010

Cecil R. Humphery-Smith, *The Phillimore
Atlas and Index of Parish Registers* Phillimore,
2003

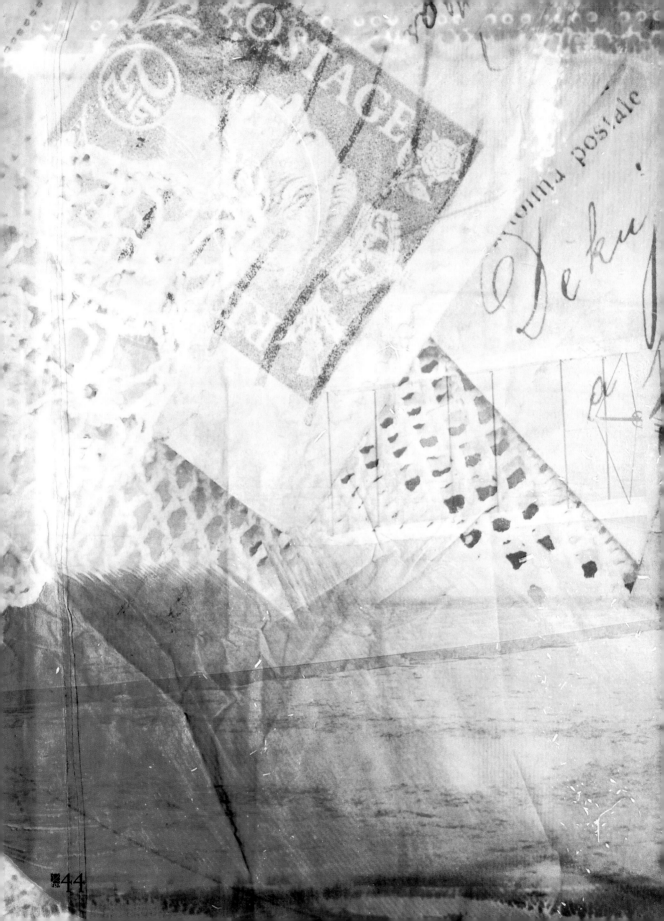

The Next Generation

Researching your Scottish family history is a rewarding adventure, which gives you the chance to explore all sorts of historic records and to visit some beautiful places too. Once you've found your Scottish ancestors, you will be sure to want to share their stories with the generations coming after you; Scottish history and heritage is treasured throughout the world to this day.

My Story ❧

*H*ere you have the opportunity to pass on any interesting facts or stories you have learned about your ancestors, or any information you would like to pass to future generations about your own life.

....
....
....
....
....
....
....
....
....

Place a photo, postcard
or clipping here

Place a photo, postcard
or clipping here

....
....
....
....
....
....
....
....
....

Place a photo, postcard
or clipping here

Place a photo, postcard
or clipping here

....
....
....
....
....
....
....
....
....

LOMOND

Lomond Books Ltd
Broxburn, EH52, Scotland
www.lomondbooks.com

Publisher and Creative Director: Nick Wells
Project Editor: Chelsea Edwards
Art Director: Mike Spender
Layout Design: Jane Ashley
Digital Design and Production: Chris Herbert

Special thanks to: Sara Robson, Digby Smith and Catherine Taylor

11 13 15 14 12
1 3 5 7 9 10 8 6 4 2

Created by and copyright © 2011 Flame Tree Publishing
Flame Tree is part of The Foundry Creative Media Company Ltd.
www.flametreepublishing.com

Helen Tovey (author) is currently editor of *Family Tree* magazine, and, despite her English West Country
surname, has so far discovered ancestors in the historic counties of Perthshire, Stirlingshire,
Dumfriesshire and Roxburghshire.

Picture Credits

Courtesy of Shutterstock and © the following photographers: Anyka 12; Ruth Black 22; David Burrows:
32; Fanfo: 14–15; frescomovie: 10, 36, 39; Kathleen Good 31 (t); Granite: 37; Giuseppe R: 2; Brendan
Howard 24 (b), 34; Danylchenko Iaroslav: 25; Val Lawless: 39; Andy Lidstone 24 (t); Luis Louro: 38–39;
Nikolay Okhitin: 38–39; OlgaLis: 8; Kenneth V. Pilon: 12, 33, 35; Mikhail Pogosov: 38–39; Scott Rothstein:
4–5; Elzbieta Sekowska 26; Michaela Stejskalova: 28–29, 38, 44–45; Ungor: 38; David Woods 36.
All records reproduced with the kind permission of the Registrar General for Scotland.
All tartan images are courtesy of Scottish Tartans World Register.

A CIP record for this book is available from the British Library.

ISBN 978-1-84204-283-0

Printed in China

This book was completed on

···